THE BIG PICTURE

THE GREATEST
MAN-MADE STRUCTURES

BY GRACE JONES

THE SECRET BOOK COMPANY
©2018
The Secret Book Company
King's Lynn
Norfolk PE30 4LS

ISBN: 978-1-912171-85-9

Printed in Malaysia

Written by:
Grace Jones

Edited by:
Madeline Tyler

Designed by:
Gareth Liddington

A catalogue record for this book is available from the British Library.

Images are courtesy of Shutterstock.com. With thanks to Getty Images, Thinkstock Photo and iStockphoto.

2 – Ekrem Canli, 3 – Irina Matsiash, 4 – kampolz, Ewelina Wachala, Shchipkova Elena, 5 – Mr Nai, Waj, aphotostory, prochasson frederic, Alexander Chaikin, Felix Lipov, 135pixels, r.nagy, TTstudio, Gurcharan Singh, Samual Chew, 6 – nixki, gerasimov_foto_174, shootmybusiness, 7 – Andrew Dunn, Keiki, 8 – Pius Lee, Asier Villafranca, 9 – Kane Rix, WitR, nimograf, 10 – Rvector, Fedor Selivanov, wikicommons, 11 – Notyourbroom, aphotostory, 12 – givaga, matsabe, Carole Raddato, 13 – Walters Art Museum, nanmulti, Zoran Karapancev, Ekrem Canli, 14 – Mary Lane, Alexander Chaikin, 15 – Jane Rix, National Portrait Gallery, National Gallery of Art, 16 – Pack-Shot, ToucanWings, Les collections du chateau de Versailles, Maria Zimovich, 17 – Bartlomiej Rybacki, Takashi Images, PhotoFires, 18 – Resui Muslu, AA.VV, 19 – Albo, Txllxt TxllxT, 20 – majeczka, Everett Historical, 21 – libre de droits, Tysto, 22 – BigMac, Sean Pavone, 23 – Lewis Hine, dovla982, Nationaal Archief, 24 – Luciano Mortula – LGM, Bill Ebbesen, 25 – Calibas, Lisboa vista de Almada, 26 – Barbara185, Hpeterswald, 27 – Anny Tseng, Samuel Chew, Rtype909, Elsham, 29 – Donaldytong, Gustavo Facci, Steve Swayne, Saffron Blaze, FCG, Yann, 31 – Anton V. Tokarev.

CONTENTS

Words that look like **this** can be found in the glossary on page 30.

THE GREATEST BUILDINGS AND STRUCTURES

Buildings and structures are places that we live in. We sleep, eat, work and even worship in these places. However, many buildings and structures are more than places where we rest our heads or admire from afar.

Buildings and structures can tell us a thousand stories. They can tell us about the history, the society and the culture of places and people through their design and **engineering**. Let's go on a journey to find out about the stories that the greatest buildings and structures in the world have to tell us!

Skyscraper

House

Mosque

What is Stonehenge and what does it tell us about **prehistoric** Britain?

How were the **ancient** Egyptian pyramids built?

How long did it take to build the Great Wall of China?

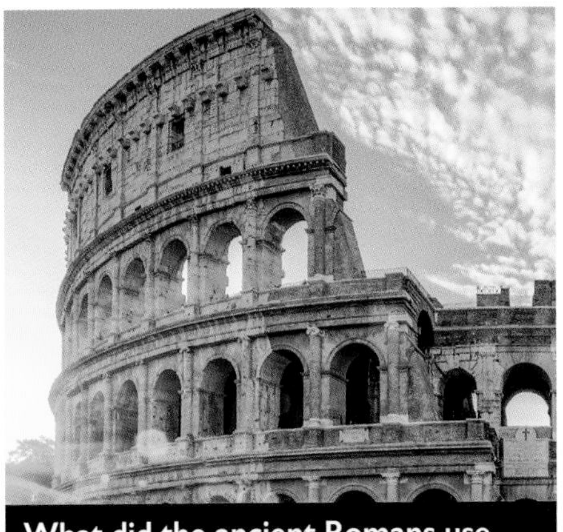

What did the ancient Romans use the Colosseum for?

What was the Tower of London built for?

Why did King Louis XIV build the Palace of Versailles?

Why is it taking so long to finish building La Sagrada Familia?

Is the Eiffel Tower the most famous structure in the world?

How tall is the Empire State Building?

Is the Golden Gate Bridge the most **iconic** bridge in the world?

How much did it cost to build the Sydney Opera House?

LET'S GO ON A JOURNEY TO FIND OUT THE ANSWERS TO THESE QUESTIONS AND MANY MORE ABOUT SOME OF THE GREATEST MAN-MADE BUILDINGS AND STRUCTURES IN THE WORLD!

STONEHENGE

Stonehenge is a collection of large stones that were **erected** in several stages over 5,000 years ago in Wiltshire, England. Historians are still not sure exactly why Stonehenge was built, but some experts believe that Stonehenge could have been used for either religious **ceremonies**, as a burial ground, or for **rituals** to mark the changing of the seasons.

Stonehenge is made from two types of stone: smaller stones known as bluestones and larger stones made from sandstone, known as sarsens. The builders of Stonehenge transported the stones hundreds of miles to the building site. Around 2150 **B.C.**, the bluestones were brought over 380 kilometres (km) from south-west Wales and, around 150 years later, the sarsen stones were carried about 32 km from north Wiltshire.

The builders only had tools made from wood, stone and rope, so no one is entirely sure how they managed to transport the stones and build such a huge structure!

Stonehenge is made of two circles; an inner circle built from bluestones, and an outer circle built from sarsens.

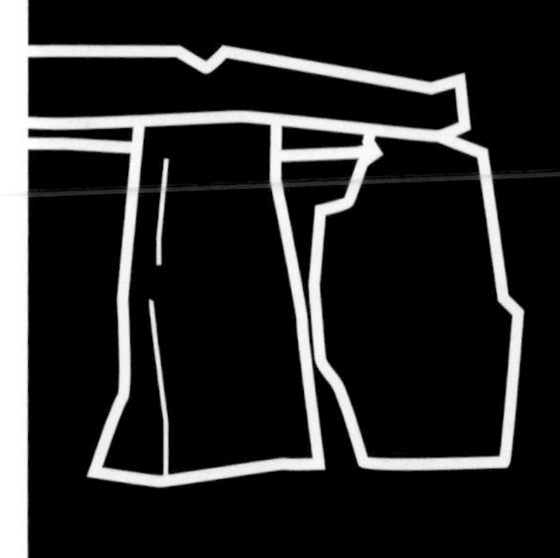

In 2013, **archaeologists** found more than 50,000 human bones buried at Stonehenge that belonged to 63 different people. Some of these bones are up to 5,000 years old. This has led many experts to believe that Stonehenge may have been built as a burial ground for ancient people. The stones may be very early gravestones that mark the graves of members of the same family, community or religious group.

Others believe that the position of the stones is linked to the position of the Sun during both the longest day of the year (the summer **solstice**) and the shortest day of the year (the winter solstice) in the Northern Hemisphere. It is thought that people would gather at Stonehenge on these days for religious ceremonies.

The entrance to the circle faces the rising Sun on the summer solstice.

Stonehenge on the Summer Solstice

GREAT PYRAMID

Thousands of years ago, the ancient Egyptians built huge structures called pyramids which have **tombs** within them where dead **pharaohs** are buried. But how did they build these amazing structures? This might seem like an almost impossible task without modern building techniques, materials and equipment such as concrete, diggers and cranes to help, but the Egyptians managed it in one of the greatest building achievements in history.

The Great Pyramid is the oldest and largest of the three pyramids of Giza and stands at 146 metres (m) tall. No one knows exactly how long it took to build, but most estimates range from around 10 to 30 years during the pharaoh Khufu's reign, which began in around 2551 B.C. Some experts believe it took between 15,000 and 40,000 people people to build the huge structure.

Pyramids of Giza

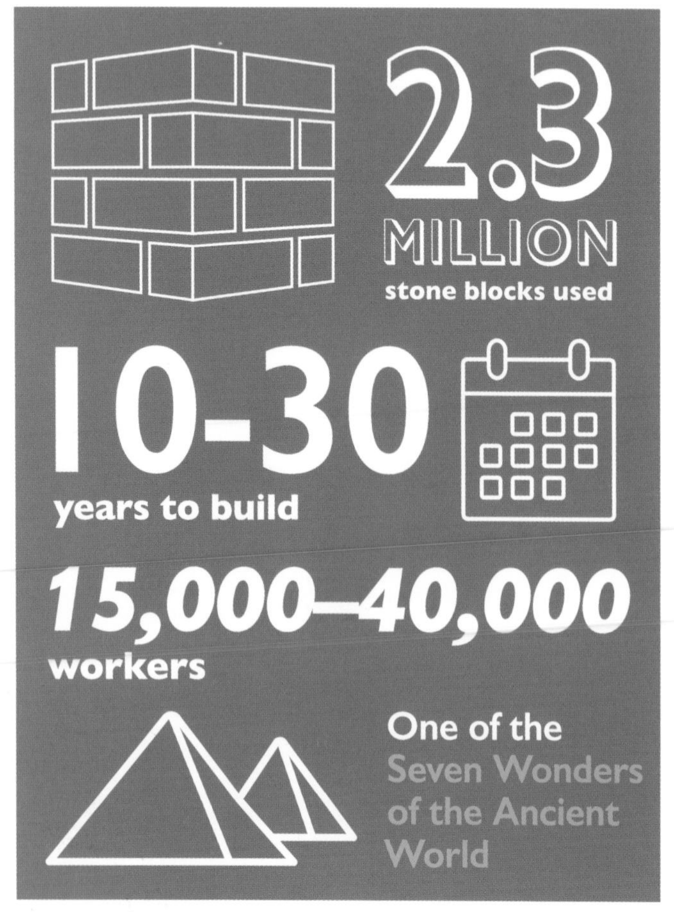

The Great Sphinx of Giza was built around the same time as the Great Pyramid.

The Egyptians had to transport large amounts of heavy building materials from faraway locations to Giza. Each block of stone had to be cut and hammered into shape near to the **quarries** where they were taken from. The blocks are thought to have been moved on land using large sledges or ramps that could be pushed or pulled by groups of workers, and then transported by boat along the River Nile.

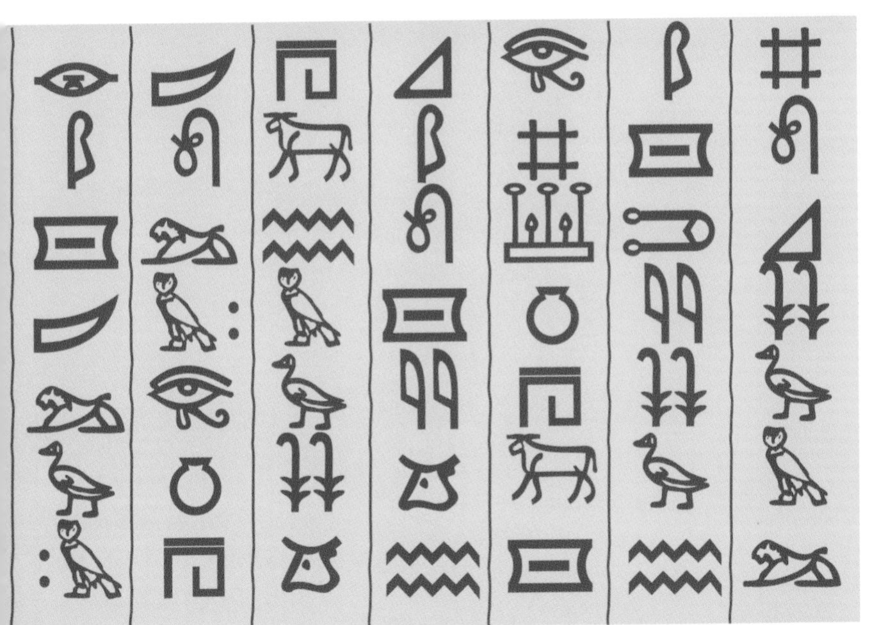

Many of the ancient Egyptian pyramids have survived until the present day and it is partly because of these amazing structures that we know so much about the language and culture of the ancient Egyptians. The pyramids have also inspired **architects** around the world. The Pyramide du Louvre in Paris, France, is a glass structure inspired by the ancient Egyptian pyramids.

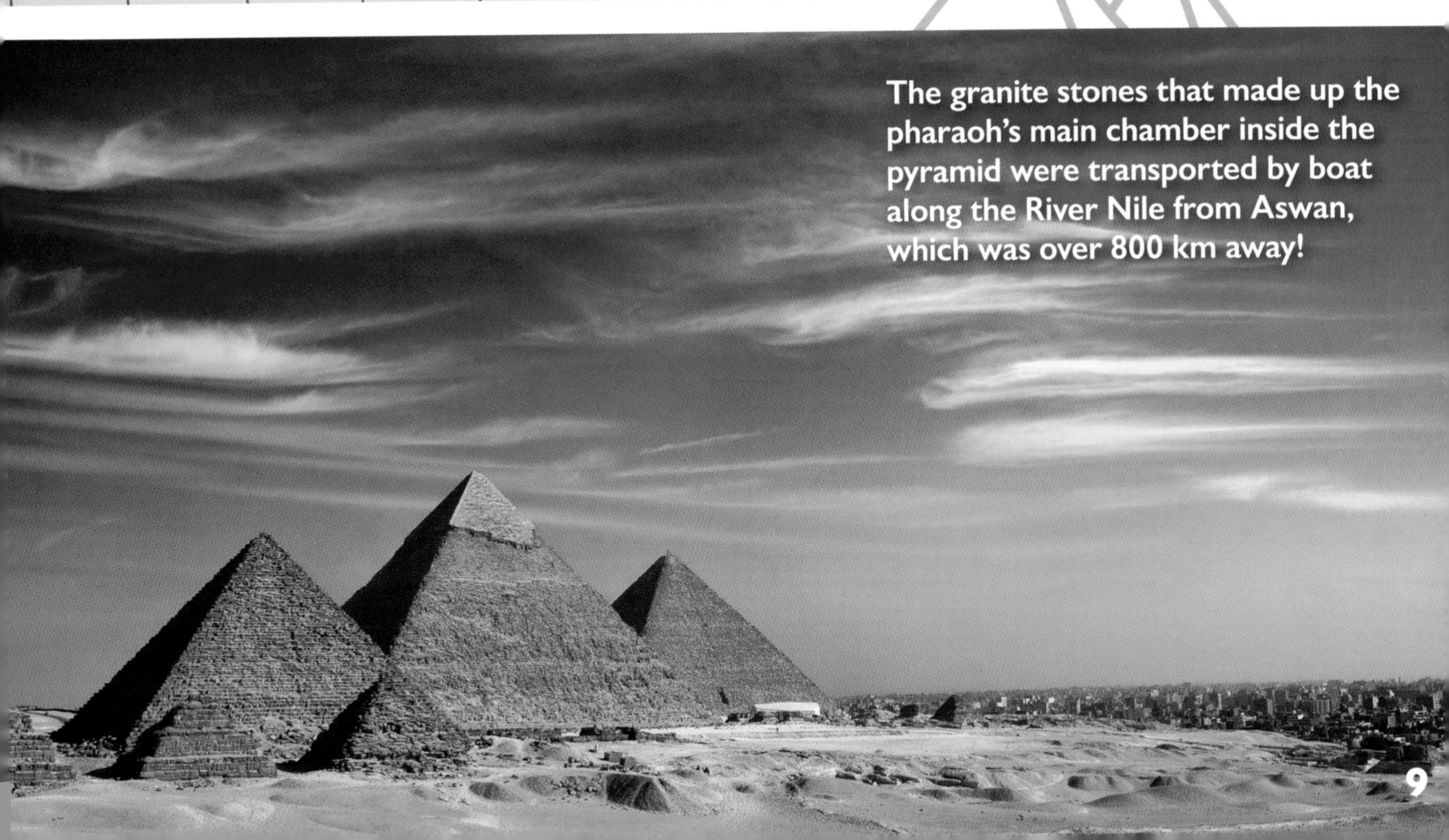

The granite stones that made up the pharaoh's main chamber inside the pyramid were transported by boat along the River Nile from Aswan, which was over 800 km away!

GREAT WALL OF CHINA

The Great Wall of China is a huge wall that stretches across China and is believed to have once been 21,000 km long. Even though parts of it are no longer standing, it is still the longest wall in the world and is the largest example of ancient architecture that still stands today.

10m

The wall receives over 10 million visitors every year.

2,300

Parts of the wall are over 2,300 years old.

7.88

The average height of the great wall is 7.88 metres.

14

The tallest point of the Great Wall is 14 metres high.

It is made from bricks, stone and soil.

7000km

Nearly one third of the original 21,000-kilometre wall has disappeared.

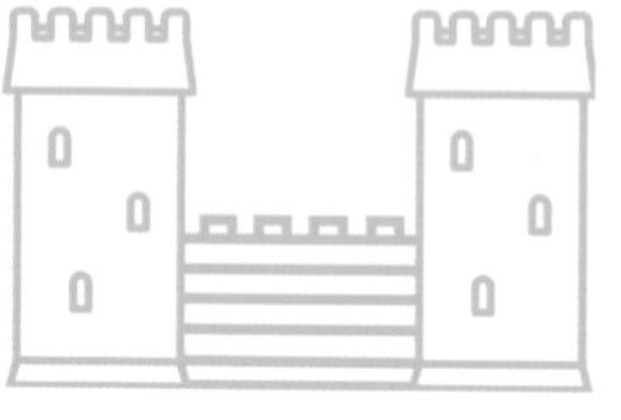

The wall was very well defended with towers and soldiers to protect the people of China from enemies.

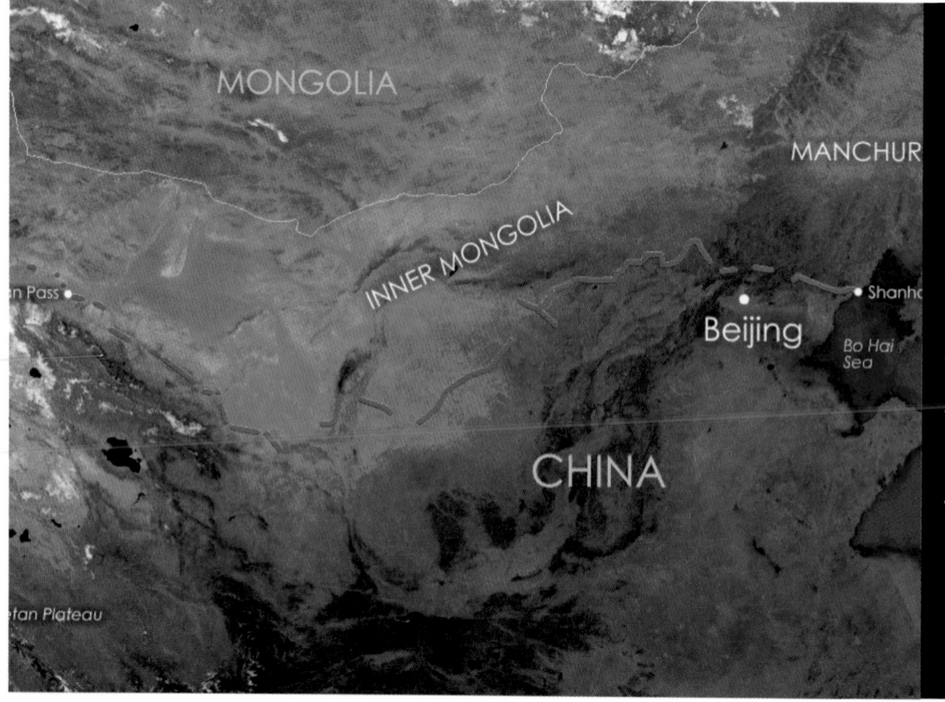

The **construction** of the Great Wall began over 2,000 years ago. It was built to defend China from **invaders** and enemy **tribes**. At first, the wall was made up of lots of separate smaller walls. Years later, all of these walls were joined together and several **watch towers** were added.

Because of its size, lots of people would have been needed to transport the materials and build the wall. Historians believe that hundreds of thousands, if not millions, of soldiers, **peasants** and criminals would have been forced to build the wall. It is thought that many people died during its construction because of the difficult working conditions, dangerous weather and the long working hours.

Parts of the Great Wall are built in deserts and near mountains, which would have made construction very difficult for the builders.

The Great Wall was built, rebuilt, made longer and repaired in many different stages over 2,000 years, but it is believed to have taken around 20 years to link up the first parts of the wall.

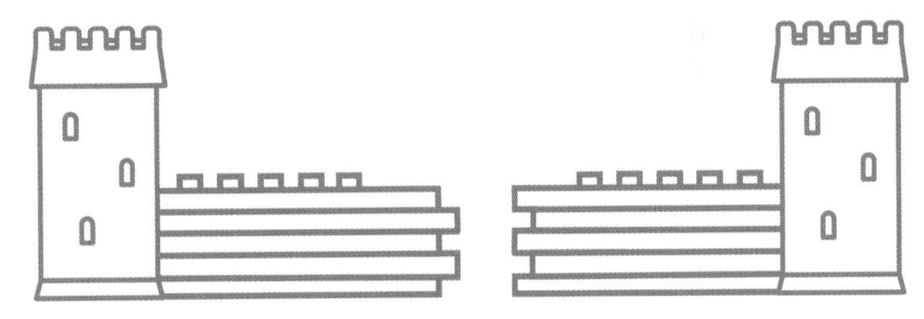

The Great Wall of China shows us the skill, effort and impressiveness of ancient Chinese **civilisations**. It is also one of the largest ancient structures in the world. It tells us a lot about ancient Chinese culture and continues to be one of the most popular tourist destinations in the world.

The Great Wall is wide enough in some places that you can drive a car on it!

COLOSSEUM

The Colosseum is a large amphitheatre built by the ancient Romans in the city of Rome, Italy between **A.D.** 70 – 80. An amphitheatre is an open, circular building with a main area in the middle used for sporting or **dramatic** events. The main area of an amphitheatre is surrounded by seating so people can watch the events.

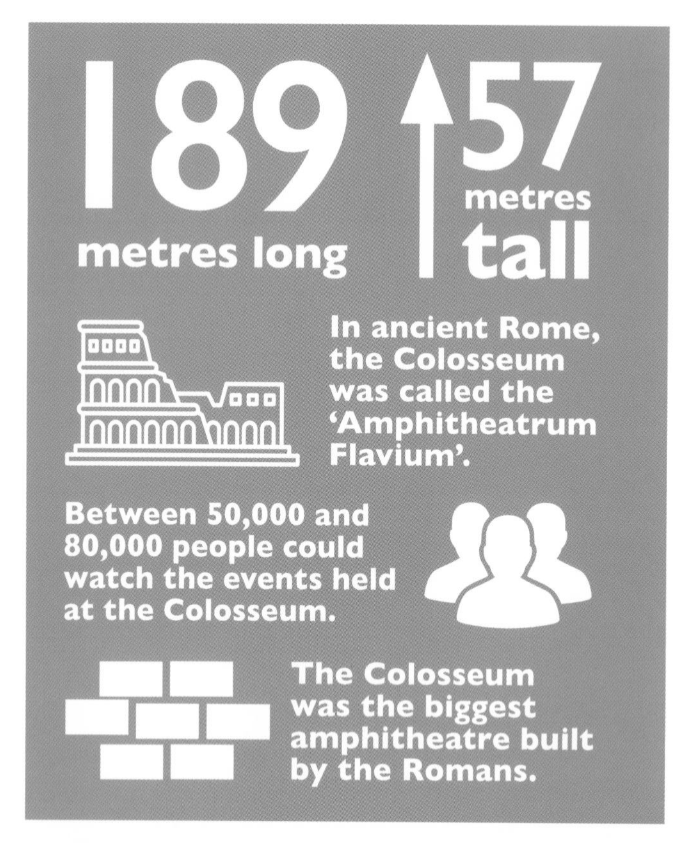

Emperor Vespasian began construction of the Colosseum in around A.D. 70–72 and Emperor Titus finished it in A.D. 80. It is made of a mixture of stone and concrete and has three floors. An estimated 100,000 prisoners and **slaves** were used to transport the building materials needed to build it, along with many skilled **stonemasons**, artists and **engineers**.

The invention of concrete sped up the building of the Colosseum. Some historians believe that if there was no concrete, the Colosseum could not have been built.

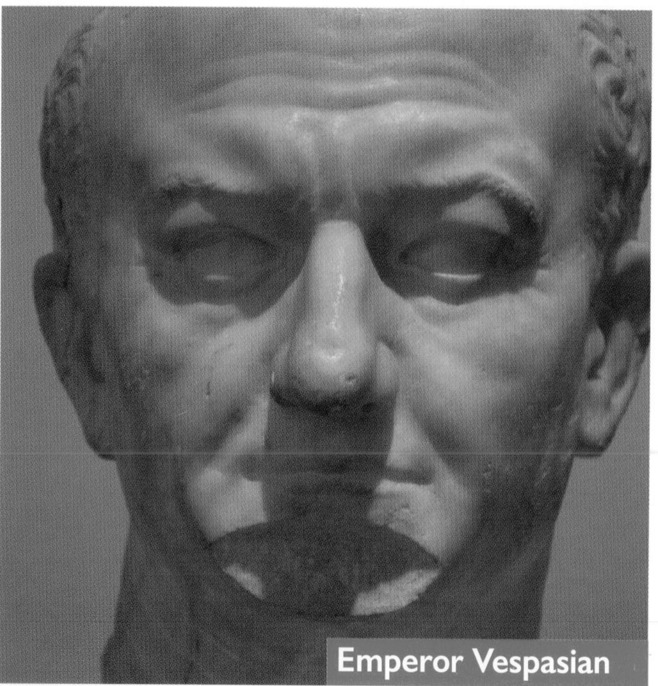

Emperor Vespasian

Emperor Titus

The Colosseum in Rome was used mostly for events involving **gladiators**. Gladiators would fight against each other to the death, until only one remained alive. Sometimes they would fight against wild animals such as lions or even bears. The Colosseum was also used for plays, the **execution** of prisoners and sometimes it was filled with water to hold sea battles.

The Colosseum is one of the most iconic buildings of ancient Rome. It was built using the latest arts, engineering and building methods of the time. Today, parts of the Colosseum are missing but it is still considered a **symbol** of the **Roman Empire** and one of the most popular tourist attractions in the world.

Criminals were sometimes sentenced to be killed by wild animals in the Colosseum, in front of an audience.

Many of the events held at the Colosseum were free for ancient Romans to enjoy.

Beijing National Stadium, China

The influence of the techniques and designs used during the building of the Colosseum can be seen in many famous stadiums that exist today.

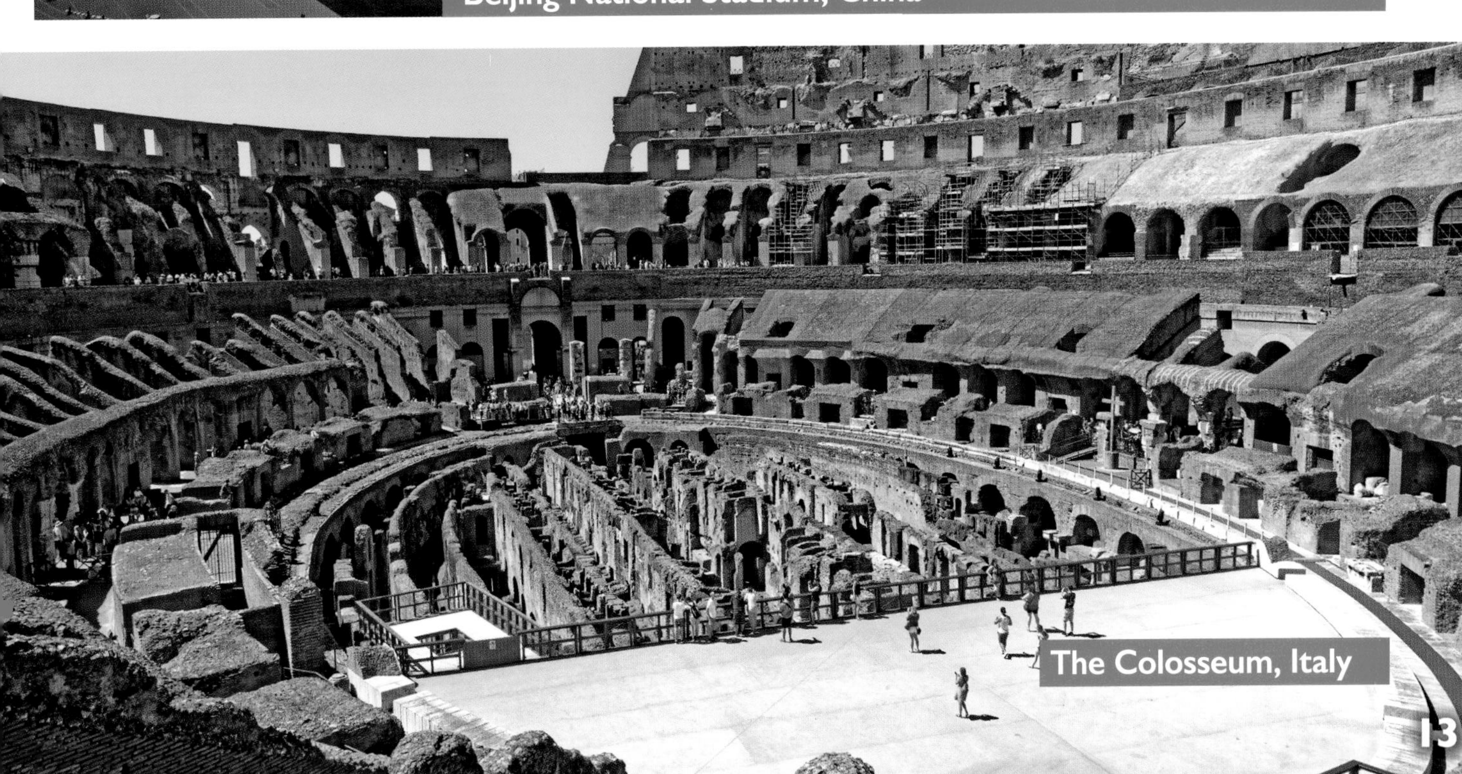

The Colosseum, Italy

TOWER OF LONDON

The Tower of London is a castle in London, England. Construction first began in A.D. 1078 and it took around 20 years to complete. Over the last 900 years, many parts of the Tower have been added and restored. Throughout history it has been used for many different things including a prison, **barracks**, and a house for the royal family.

William the Conqueror from France successfully invaded England in 1066. After this, he feared that the people of England might harm him, so he ordered the building of many castles to protect him from **rebellion**. One of these was the White Tower, which was the first part of the Tower to be built in around A.D. 1078.

White Tower

27 METRES HIGH 4.5 METRES THICK

The White Tower is over 27m high and its walls are over 4.5m thick.

Tower of London

For hundreds of years, the Tower of London was used to hold important prisoners. If they were found guilty, they would be taken to be hanged or executed in front of large crowds. Some of the most famous prisoners held in the Tower of London include Queen Elizabeth I and two of Henry VIII's wives, Anne Boleyn and Catherine Howard, who were both executed.

Anne Boleyn

Catherine Howard

The Tower of London has also been nicknamed the 'Bloody Tower' because of the gruesome end many of its prisoners met.

Elizabeth I

Elizabeth I was put in the tower by her sister Mary, but was never executed.

Today, the Tower of London is open to the public as a museum and is home to the **Crown Jewels**. As well as being an amazing **feat** of construction, it is also a place that tells many stories of England's interesting – and often gruesome – history.

The Beefeaters are guards at the Tower of London and are mainly responsible for looking after the Crown Jewels. They are also a big tourist attraction for many visitors.

PALACE OF VERSAILLES

The Palace of Versailles (say: Ver-sigh) is one of the greatest achievements in French architecture. It is a royal palace located around 20 km outside of Paris, in Versailles. The Palace was originally a royal hunting lodge and later a small castle, but King Louis XIV transformed it into a grand palace during his rule.

The Palace now contains over 2,300 rooms.

King Louis XIV began construction of his grand palace in 1661. He built the palace because he wanted to move his **court** and **government** from Paris to Versailles. He believed that by doing so he would have more control of the government and his **nobles**.

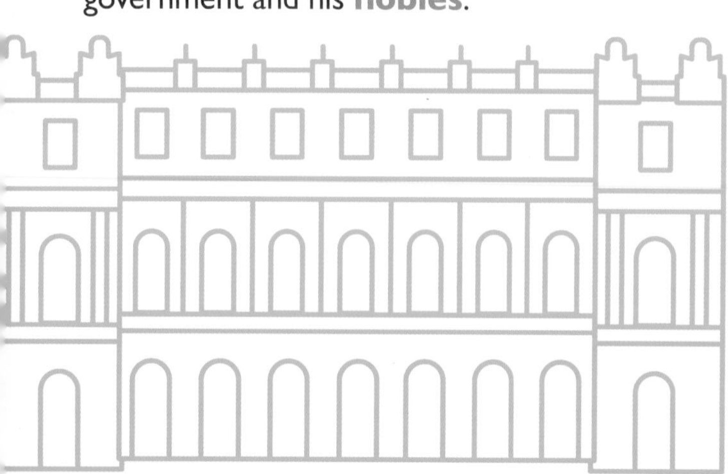

King Louis XIV moved the French court and government to Versailles in 1682.

Between 1661 and 1710, the castle was transformed into one of the grandest palaces in the world. Every part of its architecture was designed to celebrate the King. Famous architects, landscape artists and painters worked to create Louis XIV's vision of the palace and its gardens. One of the most famous rooms, the Hall of Mirrors, is over 70 m long and contains many mirrors, glass chandeliers and has a painted ceiling.

The Palace of Versailles is one of the greatest achievements in the history of France. The building of the Palace allowed Louis XIV to lead France and better control his government and his court. The Palace is now a national museum and tourists continue to be amazed by its breath–taking architecture, rooms and gardens.

The Palace of Versailles is one of the world's largest palaces and takes up 67 square km.

The kings that ruled after Louis XIV continued adding to and improving the Palace right up until the French Revolution in 1789.

Hall of Mirrors

LA SAGRADA FAMILIA

La Sagrada Familia is a large **Roman Catholic** church located in Barcelona, Spain. It was designed by the architect Antoni Gaudí. It is one of the most famous and **unique** churches in the world.

1882

The construction of the church began in 1882 and is still being worked on today.

170

When complete, the highest point of the church will be 170 m tall.

The architect, Antoni Gaudí, is buried in the church.

18

When it is finished, the church will have 18 towers.

Builders had to use paper sketches to build the church as the construction started before there were computers.

In the 19th century, a group called the Spiritual Association of Devotees of Saint Joseph planned to build a church in Barcelona for the **Holy Family**, or the 'Sagrada Familia'. They asked an architect called Francisco de Paula del Villar y Lozano to build it in 1877. However, Villar and the organisation disagreed with each other and so, in 1883, Antoni Gaudí took over its construction. Gaudí worked on it for over 33 years until his death in 1926.

Because the church is so big and important, many people, including Gaudí, called it a cathedral, even though it's a church.

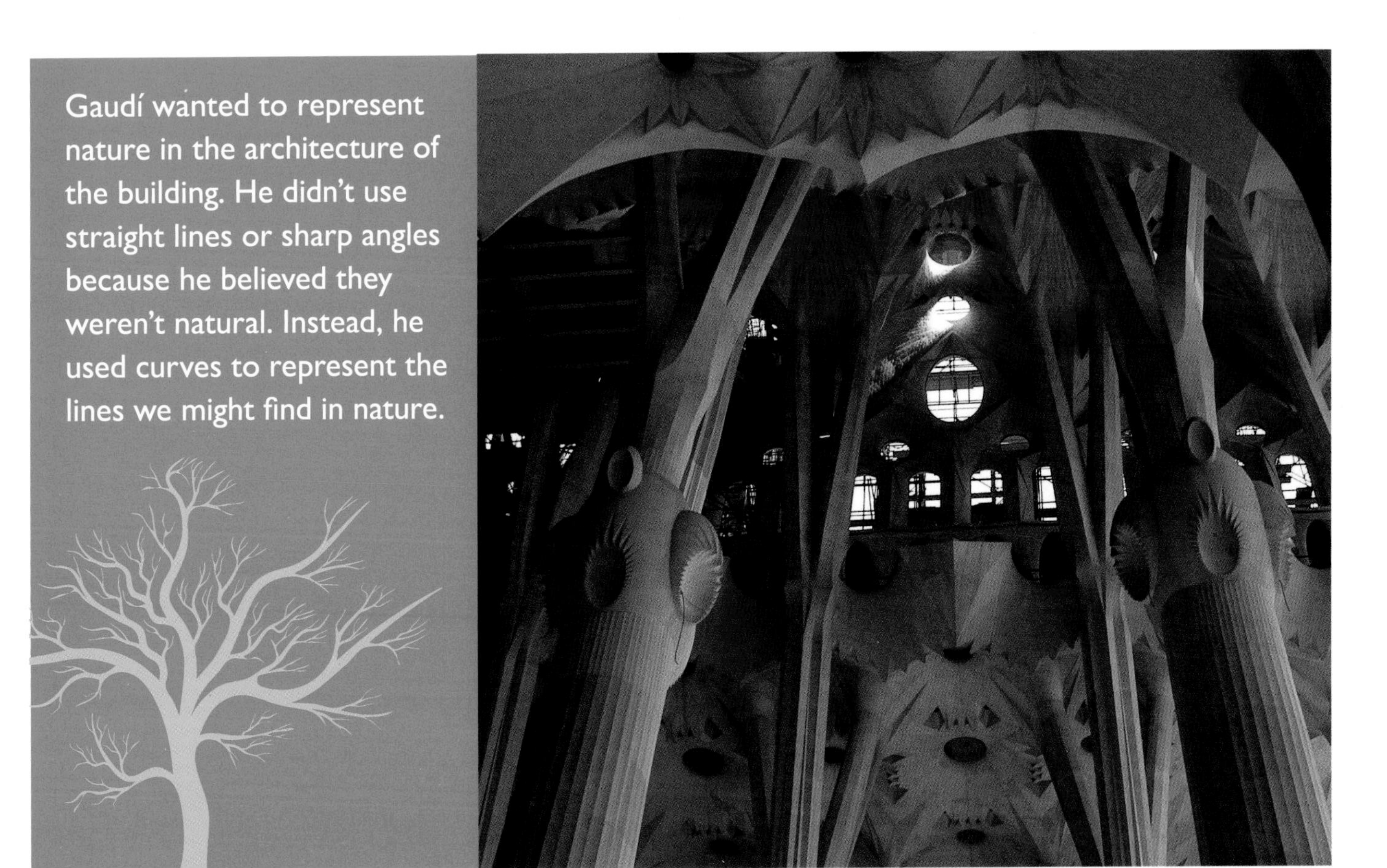

Gaudí wanted to represent nature in the architecture of the building. He didn't use straight lines or sharp angles because he believed they weren't natural. Instead, he used curves to represent the lines we might find in nature.

Some people believe that the pillars inside La Sagrada Familia look like trees. Other people think it looks like the inside of the human body.

There are 18 towers on the Church. The middle tower is for Jesus Christ, the four around it represent the **Gospels**, another the Virgin Mary and the other 12 represent the 12 **Apostles**.

Although it isn't finished, La Sagrada Familia still receives more than three million visitors every year because of its impressive architecture and Gaudí's skill in creating something so unique and artistic. Construction of the church is planned to end in 2026 to **commemorate** the 100th anniversary of Gaudí's death and to celebrate his life's work. Once it is completed, La Sagrada Familia will have taken longer to build than the Great Pyramid of Giza, which only took 20 years.

EIFFEL TOWER

The Eiffel Tower is a 324-metre-tall tower built on the Champs de Mars in Paris, France. An engineer named Gustave Eiffel designed and built the tower between 1887 and 1889. It took just two years, two months and five days to complete the huge structure that is now considered a symbol of France.

The Eiffel Tower was originally designed and built by Gustave Eiffel and his company for the 1889 **World's Fair** to celebrate the 100th anniversary of the French Revolution. It was only supposed to be there for 20 years, but it was saved and used for experiments involving communication and radio. Since then, it has been regularly improved and changed to become the most popular tourist attraction in France.

The French Revolution began in 1789. The royal family was overthrown by the French people who set up a new government called a **republic**.

6.9m

It is the most visited structure in the world, receiving over 6.9 million visitors in 2015.

The Tower is named after Gustave Eiffel – the engineer who designed it.

324

It is 324 metres tall.

41

It was the tallest man-made structure in the world for 41 years.

Some 18,000 pieces that were used to make parts of the Tower were designed, cut and put together into larger pieces in Gustave Eiffel's factory. Between 150 and 300 workers put smaller parts together to make larger ones in the factory, but some had to be assembled at the site. To erect the Tower, wooden **scaffolding** and small cranes were used.

Over 7,300 tonnes of iron and 60 tonnes of paint were used during the construction of the Eiffel Tower.

The Eiffel Tower has become one of most famous, iconic and visited structures in the world. Gustave Eiffel is also recognised as achieving amazing feats of architecture and engineering. His building method of putting together parts before erecting structures inspired the construction of many other buildings and structures such as the Statue of Liberty in New York.

EMPIRE STATE BUILDING

The Empire State Building is 381 metres tall and is located on Fifth Avenue in New York, USA. The 102 floors of the Empire State Building are used as offices, art galleries and restaurants, amongst many other things.

102

There are 102 floors.

381

It is 381 metres tall.

1931

It was the world's tallest building from 1931 until the late 1970s.

80

Tourists can sometimes see for more than 80 miles around from the top of the Empire State Building.

It got its name from the nickname for New York, which is often called the 'Empire State'.

A team of architects called Richard Harold Shreve, William F. Lamb and Arthur Loomis Harmon designed the Empire State Building in the art deco style, which was very popular at the time. Art deco is a style of architecture and decoration that focuses on elegance and glamour, and symbolises wealth and sophistication. The Empire State building is one of the most famous examples of art deco architecture. It is also an inspirational structure that, for many, symbolises American success, wealth and power.

Construction of the Empire State Building began in 1931 and took just 20 months to complete. Around 3,400 workers were involved in the construction of the building. They erected the building very quickly and, on average, four and half floors of the building were built every week.

The Empire State Building Run–Up is a race that has been held every year since 1978. Runners race each other from the ground floor up to the 86th floor using the staircases. The record time is 9 minutes and 33 seconds and was set by an Australian man called Paul Crake.

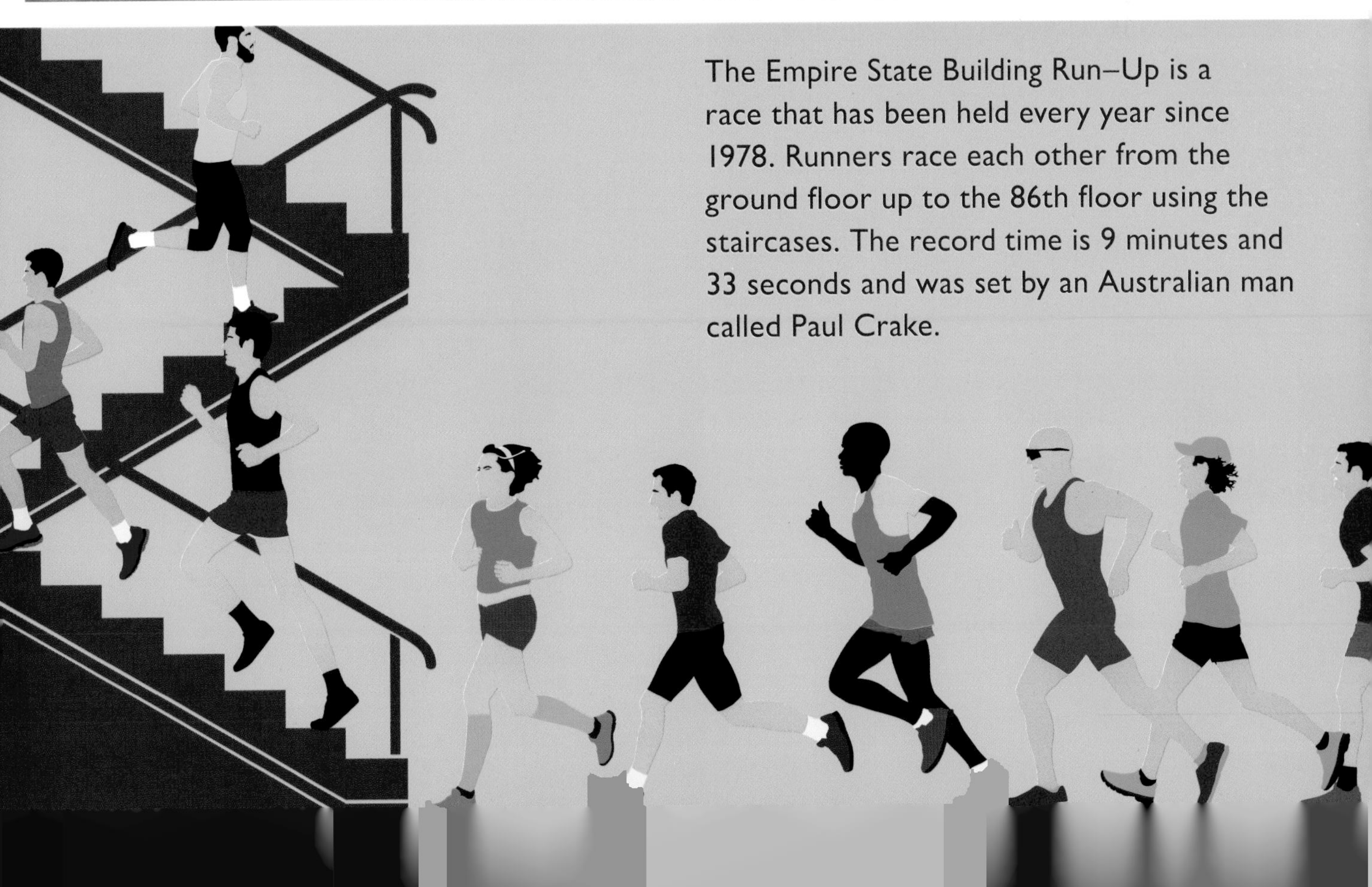

GOLDEN GATE BRIDGE

The Golden Gate Bridge is a 2.7-kilometre-long **suspension** bridge that links San Francisco, USA to Marin County, USA. The bridge is one of the most famous bridges in the world because of its recognisable and unique design. Until 1964, the Golden Gate Bridge was the longest suspension bridge in the world.

The Golden Gate Bridge was designed by Joseph Strauss, Irving Morrow and Leon Moisseiff, and construction began in January 1933. Since it was opened in 1937, over two **billion** cars have crossed the bridge with around 110,000 using it every day. The billionth driver, a dentist called Dr Arthur Molinari, crossed the bridge on the 22nd of February, 1985 and received a hardhat and champagne as a congratulations.

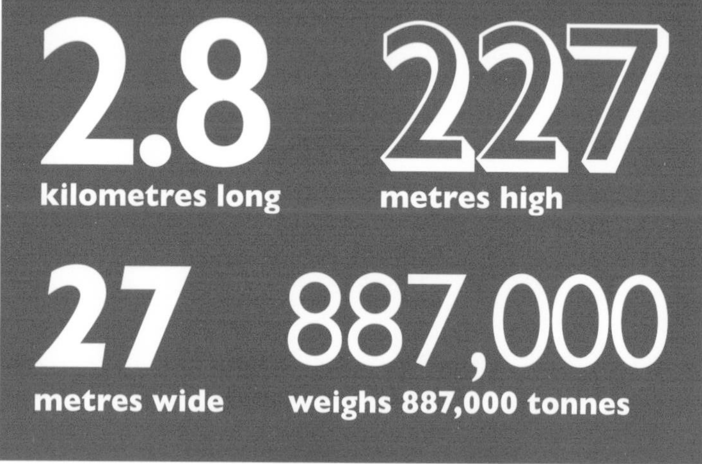

Before the bridge was built, people had to cross the river by catching a ferry. The ferry trip took around 20 minutes.

Builders and engineers started with the two towers at either end of the bridge: one was built on land and the other was over 300 m out into the water. Rough waters, strong winds and thick fog made the building of the bridge very difficult, but they finally finished it four years later in 1937. Since its opening, the bridge has been closed due to bad weather only three times.

35m

The bridge was completed on time and within budget. It cost 35 million dollars to build.

70,000

Over 70,000 tonnes of steel were used in the making of the bridge.

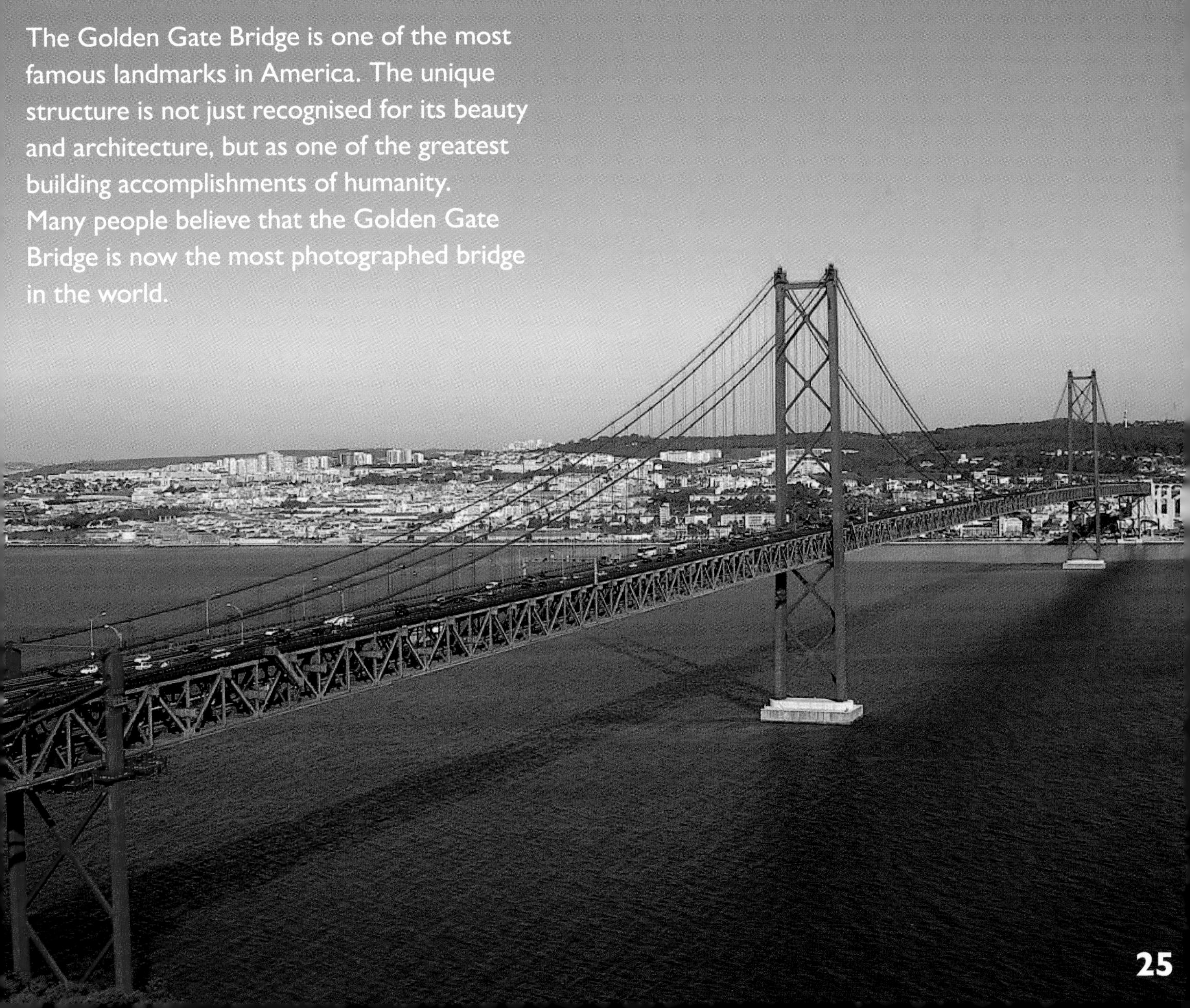

The Golden Gate Bridge is one of the most famous landmarks in America. The unique structure is not just recognised for its beauty and architecture, but as one of the greatest building accomplishments of humanity. Many people believe that the Golden Gate Bridge is now the most photographed bridge in the world.

SYDNEY OPERA HOUSE

The Sydney Opera House is an arts centre located in Sydney, Australia. It includes many venues that host around 1,500 different performances every year. The building is famous for its unique and modern style of architecture.

The Sydney Opera House's venues include:
- Concert Hall
- Joan Sutherland Theatre
- Drama Theatre
- Playhouse
- Recording Studio

1 million roof tiles

120 metres wide

183 metres long

102m Cost 102 million Australian dollars to build

6,225 square metres of glass

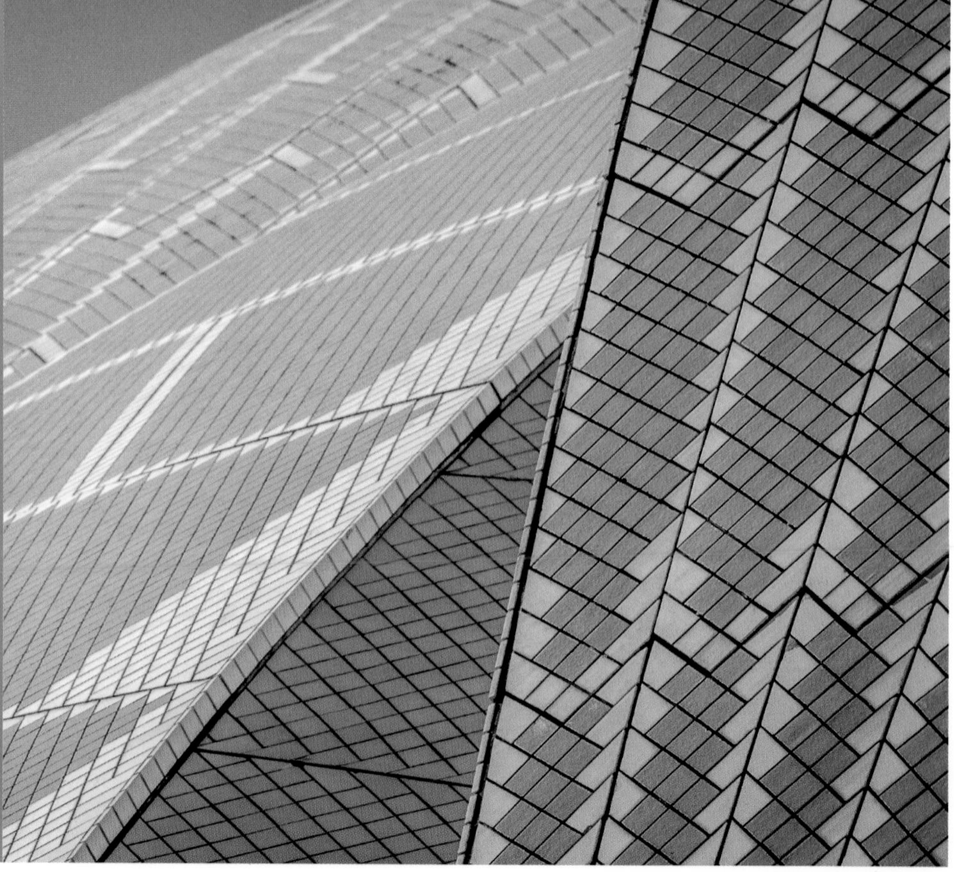

In 1956, the Australian government decided to build the Sydney Opera House. An international competition was held where architects from all over world could enter their designs. Over 233 designs were entered, but in 1957 a Danish architect called Jørn Utzon was announced the winner. Jørn Utzon's design became the Sydney Opera House that stands today.

In 1959, construction of the building began with a workforce of over 10,000 people. The 'sails' at the top of the building were each built using three huge tower cranes that were specially made in France and cost 100,000 Australian dollars each. The building was finally opened to the public 14 years later in 1973. Queen Elizabeth II formally opened the building and a large crowd came to watch the ceremony.

The top parts of the building represent a fleet of sails on Sydney Harbour, which is what the Opera House is directly next to.

Since it opened, the Sydney Opera House has had over 88,000 performances with over 35 billion people in attendance. It is the number one tourist attraction in Australia because of its unique architecture and the many events that are held there every year.

TIMELINE: THE GREATEST BUILDINGS AND STRUCTURES

2551 B.C.: Around this time, construction began on the **Great Pyramid** at Giza.

2500 B.C.: The first stages of **Stonehenge** were built.

770–476 B.C.: The first parts of the **Great Wall of China** were built.

A.D. 70–80: Construction began on the Colosseum.

1078: Building work started on the **Tower of London.**

1661: The Palace of Versailles started to be built.

1882: Building began on **La Sagrada Familia.**

1889: Construction began on the **Eiffel Tower.**

1931: Building work started on the **Empire State Building.**

1933: Construction began on the **Golden Gate Bridge.**

1959: Building began on the **Sydney Opera House.**

MORE GREAT BUILDINGS AND STRUCTURES

The Parthenon – An ancient temple in Athens, Greece, that is around 2,400 years old.

Christ the Redeemer – 30–metre–tall statue of Jesus Christ in Rio de Janerio, Brazil.

Burj Khalifa – The building in Dubai, United Arab Emirates, was opened in 2010 and is the tallest structure in the world.

The Tower of Pisa – Sometimes called the Leaning Tower of Pisa because of its tilt. It is over 600 years old and is one of the most tilted structures in the world.

The Petronas Towers – The towers are a symbol of Kuala Lumpur, Malaysia, and were the tallest in the world from 1998 until 2004.

Taj Mahal – A white marble **mausoleum** in Uttar Pradesh, India. It was built between 1632 and 1653 with the help of around 1,000 elephants!

GLOSSARY

A.D.
"anno domini" – in the year of the Lord. Used in the Christian calendar to mark dates after Jesus's birth
ancient
belonging to the very distant past
Apostles
12 followers of Jesus Christ
archaeologists
historians who study buried ruins and ancient objects in order to learn about human history
architects
people who design buildings
barracks
a building or buildings where soldiers live
billion
one thousand million
B.C.
meaning 'before Christ', it is used to mark dates that occurred before the starting year of Christian calendars
ceremonies
formal occasions celebrating achievements, people, or religious or public events
civilisations
the societies, cultures and ways of life of certain areas
commemorate
to celebrate or show respect for an event or a person
construction
the act or process of building something
court
people who formally assist a king or queen
Crown Jewels
a collection of precious jewellery, metalwork and clothes worn by the kings and queens of England
dramatic
relating to drama or acting
engineering
the activities of an engineer
engineers
people who design and build machines
erected
built in an upright position
execution
the act of putting someone to death
feat
a thing that is difficult to achieve
gladiators
people in ancient Rome who were trained to fight people and animals in an arena
Gospels
Jesus Christ's life and teachings recorded in the first four books of the New Testament of the Bible
government
the group of people with the authority to run a country and decide its laws
Holy Family
the baby Jesus, the Virgin Mary, and Joseph
iconic
widely recognised or famous
invaders
people that attack a country or an area in order to control it
mausoleum
a large building that holds a tomb inside
nobles
people of high rank
peasants
poor land workers who belonged to the lowest social class
pharaohs
kings or queens of ancient Egypt
prehistoric
any period of history that occurred before the presence of writing
quarries
large, man-made holes in the ground where natural building materials such as stone and sand are dug from
rebellion
when people fight against their government, leader or ruler
republic
a nation where the government is elected by the people

rituals
a series of ordered actions that take place during religious ceremonies
Roman Catholic
relating to the Roman Catholic faith, which is a branch of Christianity
Roman Empire
the lands and territories controlled by ancient Rome
scaffolding
a temporary structure that keeps something in place
Seven Wonders of the Ancient World
seven ancient structures of the world that are considered to be the most important
slaves
people who are legally owned by other people
solstice
two times of the year when the Sun reaches its highest or lowest point in the sky
stonemasons
people who cut and build with stone
suspension
to hang or be attached to something above rather than being supported from below
symbol
a thing that represents something else, usually a physical object that represents something non-physical
tombs
places for the burial of the dead
tribes
groups of people linked together by family, society, religion or community
unique
being the only one of its kind
watch towers
tall towers which help people see other people coming from far away
World's Fair
an international exhibition of scientific, industrial and artistic achievements of different countries

INDEX